LEARNING RESOURCE CENTRE
READING COLLEGE AND SCHOOL OF ART & DESIGN
KINGS ROAD, READING RG1 4HJ
0118 967 5060

Return on or before the last date stamped below.

Pu   Agency

Acknowledgements
Cover: © *PA Photos*
Photos: pp. 2, 4 © *PA Photos; pp. 7, 21* © *Redferns; p. 15* © *Alpha; p. 13* © *Corbis; pp. 21, 24, 27* © *London Features.*

Every effort has been made to trace copyright holders of material reproduced in this book. Any rights not acknowledged will be acknowledged in subsequent printings if notice is given to the publisher.

Orders: please contact Bookpoint Ltd, 130 Milton Park, Abingdon, Oxon OX14 4SB. Telephone: (44) 01235 827720, Fax: (44) 01235 400454. Lines are open from 9.00 – 6.00, Monday to Saturday, with a 24 hour message answering service. Email address: orders@bookpoint.co.uk

British Library Cataloguing in Publication Data
A catalogue record for this title is available from The British Library

ISBN 0 340 84875 8

First published 2002
Impression number   10 9 8 7 6 5 4 3 2 1
Year   2007 2006 2005 2004 2003 2002

Typeset by SX Composing DTP, Rayleigh, Essex.
Printed in Great Britain for Hodder & Stoughton Educational, a division of Hodder Headline Plc, 338 Euston Road, London NW1 3BH by The Bath Press Ltd.

Contents

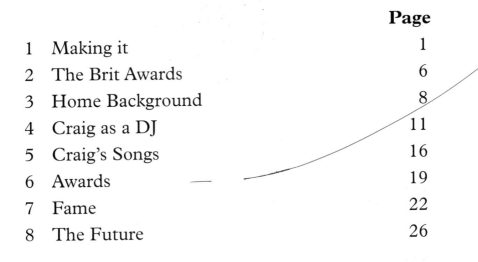

1 Making it

Craig David is a nice guy.
He never gets a bad press.
You don't read about him
getting into fights, taking drugs,
or trashing his hotel room.
Craig doesn't smoke.
He prefers drinking Coca-Cola to alcohol.

Some pop stars like the scruffy look.
Craig is not one of these.
He dresses neatly in a casual style.
He comes across as quiet and cool.
He is friendly to his fans.
He is polite to the press.

Craig was named Favourite UK Newcomer at the Capital
FM London Awards in 2000.

Craig is always willing to talk
about his music.
It is the most important thing in his life.
He calls it Fusion and says it is
a mixture of styles.
It is a blend of all kinds of music –
R&B, pop and hip-hop,
as well as garage and dance music.

Craig's music appeals to all ages.
At his concerts there are people
aged from 7 to 70.
He says he wants to appeal to
old and young in different ways.
Yet, until not so long ago, many people
had never heard of Craig David.

Late in 2000 he began to get publicity.
He won three MOBO awards.
(Music of Black Origin.)
They were for Best Newcomer,
Best R&B Act and Best UK Single.
The award-winning single was 'Fill Me In'.

Craig at the 2000 MOBO Awards in London.

In December of that year
Craig had his first solo tour.
It started off in Plymouth,
next to his home town of Southampton.
He got rave reviews from the press.
His fans turned out in force.
One of them said, 'He is just so talented.
The stage looked amazing,
he looked gorgeous,
but most of all his singing
was out of this world!'

Craig was building up a big following.
UK tours in February and March 2000
took in all the major cities.
His concerts were a sell-out.

2   The Brit Awards

At the Brit Awards in January 2001
Craig was nominated for six awards.
He did not win even one.
Robbie Williams swept the board that time.
But Craig did not act like a loser.
He won a lot of respect for the way
he behaved that night.
He did not get upset or lose his cool.
He did not say anything to spoil the show.

Sir Elton John was full of praise for him.
He said, 'If there's a better singer
than Craig David in England today,
then my name's Margaret Thatcher.'
The press also took notice of Craig.
He got a lot of publicity.
Being nominated for six awards
meant that Craig was already a success.
Now he was on his way to the big time.

Robbie Williams at the 2001 Brit Awards.

3 Home Background

Craig is of mixed race.
He does not see this as being a problem.
To him it is another part
of the 'fusion' in his life.
His father is black and comes from Grenada.
His mother is white and is from Southampton.
Craig was born in the hospital there
on 5 May 1981.

When Craig was eight, his parents split up.
But they stayed friends and
Craig didn't feel that he suffered
in any way through it.
His mum and dad made sure
that he had a happy childhood.
Both gave him love and support.
Each had a part to play in his success.

Craig's father was in the music business too.
He played bass guitar in a group
called the Ebony Rockers.
He taught Craig to enjoy reggae.
He sent Craig for lessons
to play classical guitar.
From an early age Craig's dad took him
to West Indian clubs.
There Craig met local DJs.
He picked up ideas by watching them perform.
Later Craig worked in these clubs himself.

Craig's father was quite strict.
He made sure Craig did not get into any trouble
on the estate where they lived.
Craig's mum was more easy-going.
He could get round her
if he really wanted to do something.
She let him go to clubs and do his own thing
from a young age.
She trusted Craig to behave well.
He grew up with respect for women.

His mum was a fan of Terence Trent D'Arby.
She also liked Michael Jackson
and Stevie Wonder.
Craig grew up listening to these singers.
In his teens he spent hours in his bedroom
writing his own songs.
It was his mum who made him
send one of these in for a competition.

He wrote the words for 'I'm Ready'
to music by the group Damage.
Craig won the competition.
As a prize his song was used on the B-side
of Damage's single 'Wonderful Tonight'.
This record made it to Number 3 in the charts.

4   Craig as a DJ

At the age of 14, Craig was already a DJ.
He was playing his favourite records
on a local pirate radio station.
This was PCRS
(People's Choice Radio Station).
He says it was a bit scary at times.
He was afraid the studio would be raided
and his records taken.
At that time he liked a mixture of
R&B and hip-hop.

Craig started out as a DJ by going to clubs
with his father's friend.
This friend was called DJ Flash.
Flash let him act as MC in the clubs.
Craig says that this gave him confidence.
It helped him later,
with performing in front of a crowd.

Once, when Craig was at a youth club disco,
he saw that the DJ was just playing records.
He wasn't saying much.
He couldn't connect with the audience.
Craig picked up the mike
and started chatting.
He got the crowd to respond.
He says that he first started writing songs
by making up words to use as chat
to Jungle music.

Soon Craig was getting his own
Friday night gigs at the local club Juice.
Here his winning song 'I'm Ready'
became very popular with the clubbers.
Mark Hill, half of the production duo
called Artful Dodger, heard the track.
He asked Craig to come over to his studio.

Craig was really pleased.
Here was a chance to try out
some of the other songs he had written.
The two hit it off right away.
They liked to bounce ideas off each other.

Mark Hill, who is half the production duo
called Artful Dodger.

Soon Craig and Mark began
to write songs together.
They brought together two music styles –
Craig's R&B and Mark's Garage.
As well as writing songs together,
Craig and Mark worked as a team on radio.
They had their own Garage show
on Capital FM.

Their first joint single was called
'What Ya Gonna Do'.
Later they changed the title to 'Rewind'.
Mark really liked Craig's voice.
He wanted Craig to sing solo on the track.
The single was a big hit.
It led to Craig being signed up
by Wildstar Records.
The single also did well in the USA.
American producers such as Puff Daddy
began to take notice of Craig.

'Fill Me In', the follow-up to 'Rewind',
went straight into the charts at Number 1.
Craig was still only 19 years old.
He was the youngest British male solo artist
to have a Number 1 hit.

Craig had a Number 1 hit with the single, 'Fill Me In'.

5 Craig's Songs

The fans like Craig's songs
because they are catchy.
They are easy to sing and great to dance to.
You can relate to the words of the lyrics.
The title of *Born to Do It,*
Craig's first album,
is the story of his life so far.
The title came from Craig's love of the film
Willy Wonka and the Chocolate Factory.

In the film, a child asks the candy man,
'Why? How does he do it?'
The candy man says,
'Sometimes you can't explain.
Do you ask a fish how it swims?
Do you ask a bird how it flies?
No, Siree, you don't.
They do it because they were born to do it.'

Craig thinks this makes perfect sense.
He says, 'The title was my way of saying
I was born to write and sing songs.'

'Walking Away', the third single from this album,
was released on 20 November 2000.
It went straight into the charts at Number 3.
'Rendezvous', the fourth single,
came out in March 2001.

Craig's favourite track from
the album is 'Fill Me In'.
He thinks the lyrics
are the best he has written.
He says all the tracks are very different.
There are different songs
for different moods.
'Time to Party' is a straight club track.
'You Know What' tells what it's like
to be dumped.
'Can't Be Messing 'Round' is about
saying no to other girls
when you have a girlfriend.
'Once in a Lifetime' is a track for chilling out to.

Craig's songs paint a picture
of what it's like to be a young person
in the 21st century.
They tell about the pain of falling in love.
They express the doubts that young people have
as they join the adult world.

6 Awards

Soon after the Brit Awards
Craig went on to great success.
At the BT EMMAs
(Ethnic Multi-cultural Media Awards),
he won the Best British music award
with 'Fill Me In' / 'Walking Away'.

In February 2001, he was on stage at the
Time and Life building in New York City.
There he sang alongside Willa Ford.
They were two of the 20 young people picked
as 'Twenty Teens Who Will Change the World'.
The teenagers came from many different fields.
Craig and Willa got special awards for music.

As if this wasn't enough, in May 2001
Craig won three Ivor Novello Awards.
One for Best Contemporary Song,
one for The Dance Award,
and one for Songwriter of the Year.

Craig said it was 'off the hook'
to share the songwriting award with Mark Hill.
It made up for the Brit Awards,
when he came away empty-handed.
It was turning out to be his year after all.

Craig performing with the Artful Dodger. Their songwriting talents were recognised at the Ivor Novello Awards, when Craig won three awards, including one for Songwriter of the Year.

7 Fame

Fame does not seem
to have changed Craig David.
He admits that he likes being centre stage.
Even as a little boy he loved performing.
He wanted to be a star from the age of five.
At school Craig was in lots of plays
and often got the lead part.
He says the best thing about being famous
is being in the limelight.
There is nothing he enjoys more
than performing.

On the downside he says there is a lot
of jealousy in the world of showbiz.
He is getting good at sussing out fakes.
People who never used
to give him the time of day
now want to be his best friend.

Girls who refused to go out with him once
now ask him for dates.

Speaking about girls,
in 2001 there was no one special in his life.
He hadn't been out with anyone famous.
There was a rumour that he had sent
a romantic text message to Samantha Mumba.
Craig says he understands
why celebs often date other celebs.
They're the only people who really understand
the job they're doing.
They understand the pressures.
They learn to cope with having
their private lives written about in the papers.

Craig's feet are still firmly on the ground.
He says that if people
keep telling you you're wonderful,
it can be very bad for you.
You start to believe you're something special.
Craig takes it all with a pinch of salt.
He is proud of what he's done
but he doesn't take it for granted.

Craig enjoys entertaining his fans. Here
he is at the Rockefeller Center in
New York.

He doesn't mind
if people recognise him in the street.
He is happy to sign autographs for fans.
Craig thinks it matters how you look.
He wants to make a good impression.
He says, 'People do notice what you're wearing.
I'm not a fashion victim but I like
to make sure I look good.'

At school he was on the chubby side.
Now he eats healthy food
to keep his weight down.
He always tries to look neat and well-groomed.

Asked about the secret of getting
that big break, Craig replies,
'It all comes down to hard work.
Be cool, take things one step at a time
and never look too far ahead.
There's no point worrying about the future.
Sure, I've got goals and dreams,
but I make sure I live in the present.'

8   The Future

So what does the future hold for Craig David?
It would be hard for him to top the success
that he has already had.

To date, *Born to Do It* has sold
four million copies worldwide.
One and a half million of these
were in the UK.

The album has earned gold, platinum
and multi-platinum discs in 20 countries.

Craig in America in 2001.

Craig has had dozens of rave reviews.
The music paper *NME* said he was
'the best thing to happen
to British R&B, ever'.
Other stars besides Sir Elton John admire him.
Usher, Sisqō and Jennifer Lopez are all fans.

Some pop stars take years
to become popular in America.
Some don't make it at all.
Craig has already made it into the charts
in the USA.

The DJ-centric music magazine, *NME*
may be right.

It said: 'Craig David is set to conquer
the States in 2001
as the ideal 21st century soul boy
who was simply born to do it.'